*This book is presented to*

Master Zackary James ♥

*With love from*

Caleb and Joshua Cornish

# May You Grow In Grace

## A Gift To Welcome The New Baby

Compiled by Karen J. Carroll

Illustrated by Betty Whiteaker

The C.R. Gibson® Company, Norwalk, Connecticut

# Whispers of Maternity

O, hush, little wild bird,
trill softly your song—
The shadows are falling...the day has been long:
All purple and crimson and gold, glow the skies—
And under my heart...another heart lies!

O, hush, sportive west wind, blow soft o'er the lea
All laden with perfume and summer for me;
Blow lightly and faintly as from Southern skies—
For under my heart...a little heart lies!

O, smile on us, Heaven, bend low to us now—
The seal of your glory, place here on my brow:
For twilight is falling...the tender day dies—
And under my heart...a dearer heart lies!

*Marcia Ray*

# Message From God

*W*hen God wants an important thing done in this world or a wrong righted, he goes about it in a very singular way. He doesn't release his thunderbolts or stir up his earthquakes. He simply has a tiny baby born, perhaps in a very humble home, perhaps of a very humble mother. And he puts the idea or purpose into the mother's heart. And she puts it in the baby's mind, and then—God waits. The great events of this world are not battles and elections and earthquakes and thunderbolts. The great events are babies, for each child comes with a message that God is not yet discouraged with man but is still expecting goodwill to become incarnate in each human life.

*Edward McDonald*

*H*e will be a joy and delight to you,
and many will rejoice
because of his birth.
*Luke 1:14*

*T*each us how to bring up the child
who is to be born.
*Judges 13:8*

# Our Baby Is Born

Date _January 28th 2002_ Time _8:58pm_

Place _Misericordia Hospital - Edmonton_

Weight _9_ lbs. _4_ ozs.

Height _21½ inches_

Color of eyes _Blue_

Color of hair _Dark Brown_

Our child's name _Zachary James Sneath_

*Y*ou brought me out of the womb; you made me trust in you
even at my mother's breast. From birth I was cast upon you;
from my mother's womb you have been my God.

*Psalms 22: 9-10*

# Maternity

Within the crib that stands beside my bed
A little form in sweet abandon lies
And as I bend above with misty eyes
I know how Mary's heart was comforted.

O world of Mothers! Blest are we who know
The ecstasy—the deep God-given thrill
That Mary felt when all the earth was still
In that Judean starlight long ago!

*Anne P.L. Field*

# Let Us Go
## to the House of the Lord

We brought you to _____ church.

For a service of _____

The officiant was _____

Sponsors, witnesses and friends _____

_____

A prayer for our baby _____

_____

_____

# Little Hands

Soft little hands that stray and clutch,
  Like fern fronds curl and uncurl bold,
    While baby faces lie in such
  Close sleep as flowers at night that fold,
  What is it you would clasp and hold,
Wandering outstretched with willful touch?
  O fingers small of shell-tipped rose,
  How should you know you hold so much?
  Two full hearts beating you enclose,
Hopes, fears, prayers, longings, joys, and woes,—
    All yours to hold, O little hands!
  More, more than wisdom understands
    And love, love only knows.

*Laurence Binyon*

Lord Jesus Christ, our Lord most dear,
As thou was once an infant here,
so give this child of thine, we pray,
Thy grace and blessing day by day.
Thy saving grace on him bestow
That he in thee may live and grow.

*Fifteenth-Century Petition*

I am the bread of life.
He who comes to me will never go hungry,
and he who believes in me
will never be thirsty.

*John 6:35*

# Gifts For Our Baby

Gift           From

# Gifts For Our Baby

| Gift | From |
|------|------|
|      |      |
|      |      |
|      |      |
|      |      |
|      |      |
|      |      |
|      |      |
|      |      |
|      |      |
|      |      |
|      |      |
|      |      |
|      |      |
|      |      |
|      |      |
|      |      |
|      |      |
|      |      |
|      |      |

*This is the day
the Lord has made;
let us rejoice
and be glad in it.*

*Psalms 118:24*

# The Children

They are idols of the hearts
and of households;
They are angels of God in disguise;
The sunlight still sleeps in their tresses,
His glory still gleams in their eyes;
These truants from home and from heaven—
They have made me more manly and mild;
And I know now how Jesus could liken
The Kingdom of God to a child.

*Charles M. Dickinson*

*J*esus said to them,

"Let the little children

come to me,

and do not hinder them,

for the kingdom of God belongs

to such as these..."

And he took the children

in his arms,

put his hands on them

and blessed them.

*Mark 10:14*

# At Day's End

*I* hold you in my arms before the fire
And tell the fairy tale you love the best,
While winter twilight deepens and the first
White star comes forth to glitter in the west.

So softly do you lie against my heart
I scarcely know if it be child or flower
I cradle, till you stir and draw a breath
Of wonder at the tale, O blessed hour!

That every mother knows when at day's end
She holds her little child, a wistful ache
Co-mingling with her joy, and dreams a dream
For him and breathes a prayer for his sake!

*Adelaide Love*

*He gathers the lambs*
*in his arms*
*and carries them*
*close to his heart*

Isaiah 40:11

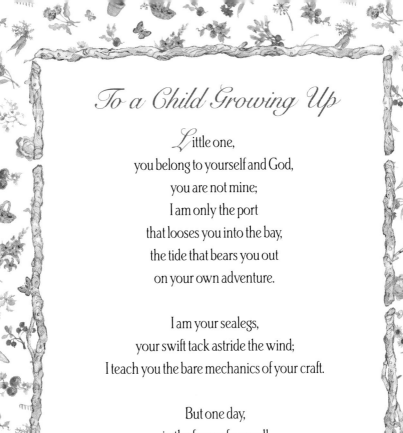

# To a Child Growing Up

*L*ittle one,
you belong to yourself and God,
you are not mine;
I am only the port
that looses you into the bay,
the tide that bears you out
on your own adventure.

I am your sealegs,
your swift tack astride the wind;
I teach you the bare mechanics of your craft.

But one day,
in the furor of a squall
or in the awful silence of a calm,
you'll find I'm not beside you at the helm;
and , if I've done my job right,
you will not be alone.

*Karen Livingston Raab*

# Rocker Full of Love

This cherry rocker: once it held
my grandmother, who cared
to rock her daughter with a song,
who knew love's joy is shared.

My mother soothed me in this chair
with gentle, loving arms;
and told me of this wondrous world,
and kept me safe from harm.

My own small daughter asks to rock.
She chants her homemade rhyme,
so snugly wrapped, in that dear chair,
with love that transcends time.

*Virginia Covey Boswell*

These are the things to cherish:
A seed and a dream and a child;
Else must the nations perish,
And earth fall away to the wild.
These are the things to nourish:
The budding of trees and youth;
So shall the grown things flourish—
Manhood and beauty and truth.

*Author Unknown*

*I* will sing of the love
of the Lord forever;
with my mouth I will make your faithfulness
known through all generations.

*Psalms 89:1*

*And the
child grew
and became strong;
he was filled with wisdom,
and the grace of God
was upon him.*

*Luke 2:40*

*. . his mother treasured*
*all these things in her heart.*

*Luke 2:51*

*D*ear Lord, make me a blessed mother for this child. Help me to encourage this child to grow and develop in every way that You planned. When I don't understand my child, please give me wisdom; when I am depressed don't let me burden this child with my problems, but fill my heart with gladness; and when I am impatient help me to remember that a child needs a lot of love and patience to develop fully. And help me, Lord, to love my child as deeply and constantly as You love each of us, for You have entrusted me with a tender and dependent person. Above all, dear Lord, help me to guide this child to find the firm foundation that comes from knowing You as Lord and Saviour.

*Karen J. Carroll*

*A* baby needs the sunshine
of his mother's love
to develop the sturdy roots
of a strong and fertile character.

*Janet C. Kaye*

*T*each me your way,
O Lord,
and I will walk
in your truth.

*Psalms 86:11*

*I* will pour out my Spirit
on your offspring...
They will spring up like grass in a meadow,
like poplar trees by flowing streams.

*Isaiah 44:3-4*

I love little children
and it is not
a slight thing
when they,
who are fresh
from God, love us.

Charles Dickens

And a little child
will lead them.

Isaiah 11:6

## Acknowledgments

The editor and publisher have made every effort to trace the ownership of all copyrighted material and to secure permission from copyright holders of such material. In the event of any question arising as to the use of any such material, the editor and the publisher, while expressing regret for inadvertent error, will be pleased to make the necessary corrections in future printings. Thanks are due to the following publishers and authors for permission to use the material indicated.

Boswell, Virginia Covey, for "Rocker Full of Love" copyright by Virginia Covey Boswell

Raab, Karen Livingston, for "To A Child Growing Up" by Karen Livingston Raab from Christian Herald Magazine, 1980.

Zondervan Bible Publishers, for all Scripture quotations used in this book. It has been taken from the Holy Bible: New International Version. Copyright 1978 by the International Bible Society. Used by permission of Zondervan Bible Publishers.